Maple Tree Press books are published by Owlkids Books Inc.
10 Lower Spadina Avenue, Suite 400, Toronto, Ontario M5V 2Z2
www.owlkids.com

Distributed in Canada by Raincoast Books
9050 Shaughnessy Street, Vancouver, British Columbia V6P 6E5

Distributed in the United States by Publishers Group West
1700 Fourth Street, Berkeley, California 94710

Dedications
For the two special people who brought so much magic into my life: my sons Andrew and Michael.
~ Helaine
For my mother, who performs magic in her own way everyday.
~ Claudia

Cataloguing in Publication Data
Becker, Helaine, 1961-
        Magic up your sleeve : amazing illusions, tricks, and science facts you'll never believe /
Helaine Becker, illustrated by Claudia Dávila.

Includes index.
ISBN 978-1-897349-75-5 (bound).--ISBN 978-1-897349-76-2 (pbk.)

        1. Magic trick--Juvenile literature. 2. Science--Miscellanea--Juvenile literature.
3. Science and magic--Juvenile literature. I. Dávila, Claudia II. Title.

GV1555.B43 2010   j793.8   C2009-905309-8

Library of Congress Control Number: 2009935532

Design: Claudia Dávila

ONTARIO ARTS COUNCIL
CONSEIL DES ARTS DE L'ONTARIO

Canada Council   Conseil des Arts
for the Arts   du Canada

We acknowledge the financial support of the Canada Council for the Arts, the Ontario Arts Council, the Government of
Canada through the Book Publishing Industry Development Program (BPIDP), and the Government of Ontario through the
Ontario Media Development Corporation's Book Initiative for our publishing activities.

The activities in this book have been tested and are safe when conducted as instructed. The author and publisher accept
no responsibility for any damage caused or sustained by the use or misuse of ideas or material featured in *Magic Up Your
Sleeve*.

Manufactured by Sheck Wah Tong Printing Press Ltd.
Manufactured in Guang Dong, China in December 2009
Job # 46157

A   B   C   D   E   F

MAGIC UP YOUR SLEEVE

Amazing Illusions, Tricks, and Science Facts You'll Never Believe

Helaine Becker

Illustrated by Claudia Dávila

MAPLE
TREE
PRESS

CONTENTS

SCIENCE STUNNERS

MATH MAGIC

SHOW-STOPPING SCIENCE

MAGICIAN'S SURVIVAL GUIDE

ENTER THE WORLD OF THE MAGICIAN

You, O Mighty Magician, have the power.

When you snap your fingers, mysterious objects appear and disappear. Wave your wand, and you make ordinary objects move. You control the forces of the universe!

At least, that's the case when you perform the magic tricks found in this book. But it doesn't end there. As you hone your mystifying powers, you'll discover the secret science behind the magic.

Focus for a bit on the science of your eyes, and you'll make printed words dance or multiply money at the drop of a dime. And with a little lesson in air pressure and temperature, you'll conjure up a ghost sure to astonish any audience.

So don your cloak and polish your wand. The power to amaze and astound is at your fingertips. *Alakazam* and *abracadabra*—prepare to unleash the magical world of science sorcery!

Getting Started

So what magic do you have up your sleeve? Before you tackle the tricks on the following pages, prepare your **Magician's Kit**. With these tools of the trade and the tips found in the **Magician's Survival Guide** (see page 58), you'll be ready to wow an audience.

Coins
(a few in each denomination)

~

Pencils

~

Handkerchief
(can be used as blindfold)

~

Drinking glasses
(plastic and glass)

~

Rubber bands

~

Paper

~

Deck of cards

~

Table and long tablecloth

Look for these wands to see how each trick is rated

easy   medium   difficult

EYE SEE!

Do they need to see it to believe it? Leave your audience guessing with this sense-sational trick!

THE BOUNCING APPLE

Throw an apple onto the ground. Instead of going "splat," it bounces high in the air. How? Only you, the Fabulous Fruitzini, know for sure!

YOU'LL NEED

apple

~

table with long tablecloth

~

chair

BEFORE THE SHOW:

This trick is all about timing, so practice before you perform it.

1 Sit down behind your table with your chair at a slight angle. Show the audience your apple.

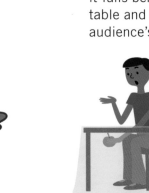

2 Drop the apple so that it falls behind the table and out of the audience's sight.

3 Quietly catch the apple below the tabletop in your other hand.

4 At the same time, tap your heel on the floor to imitate the sound of an apple hitting the ground.

TAP!

5 Wait a split second and then toss the apple up into the air. Catch it in your hand.

What's Going On?

Your audience just fell victim to a sensory illusion—a trick that fools your senses. When your audience hears the bounce (a.k.a. your foot tap) and sees the rebounding fruit, those cues give the impression that the apple really bounced. So while common sense says an apple can't bounce, the audience's senses tell a different story!

Bounce These Around Your Brain

Cold balls aren't as bouncy as warm ones. Why? Balls bounce because they are made of flexible materials like **rubber** that change shape. When they hit the ground, balls squish and flatten a bit. How much they squish and how quickly they return to their original shape determines how high they bounce. A cold ball is usually less squishable, so it won't have the same bounce as a warm ball.

The **world record** for bouncing a ball on your head was set by a Cuban man named Erick Hernandez in 2007. He bounced a soccer ball off his noggin 350 times in one minute!

A red kangaroo can travel 8 m (25 ft.) in a **single leap**. It can also bounce 1.8 m (6 ft.) high!

You only hear a **sound** when its vibrations bounce against your eardrum.

BRING ON THE GHOSTS

Charm the dead back to life with this sure-to-spook trick.

THE WRITE STUFF

Make ghostly messages appear out of thin air to freak out your friends.

BEFORE THE SHOW:

Two hours before your performance, put the water into the cup or small mixing bowl. Slowly add the salt and stir—don't worry if some of it doesn't dissolve. Let cool. Dip the cotton swab into the salty water. Lightly write "Boo!" in large letters on a sheet of paper with the salt solution. Let dry.

1 Tell your audience that you have conjured up a ghost. The freaky phantom has a message for the audience. Hold up the sheet of paper.

2 Explain that the ghost, being invisible, used invisible ink. But you, Great Ghost-o-nator, can reveal its secret message with your magic wand. Hold up your wand—which is nothing but an ordinary pencil.

3 Lay the sheet of paper flat on a table. Using the side of the pencil point, rub across the entire page. The word "Boo!" will miraculously appear!

YOU'LL NEED

Magician's Kit (see page 7)

~

15 mL (1 tbsp.) hot tap water

~

15 mL (1 tbsp.) salt

~

small cup or mixing bowl

~

spoon

~

cotton swab

PERFORMANCE TIP

Try other messages: "I see you!" or "Hi (your friend's name here)!" Or make up your own phantom messages.

What's Going On?

As you wrote, salt was transferred to the paper. When the water evaporated, it was left behind tiny white crystals, which are hard to see on the page. More of the pencil's graphite will crumble onto the rough salt than onto the smooth paper. So your audience sees the message!

Get the Message?

In ancient China, diplomats wrote **secret messages** on tiny pieces of silk. The silk was rolled up and stuffed inside a small ball of wax. Then a courier would swallow the ball. Once the courier made it past the enemy, he could "pass" the message to its recipient...after a trip to the washroom!

In 1864, a 16-year-old American teen named Henry Solomon Wellcome invented and sold **invisible ink** to help people share top-secret messages with one another. The ink was, in fact, just lemon juice!

Thanks to new technology, ghostly messages written on **ancient scrolls** might be deciphered at last. A volcano eruption buried the town of Pompeii in Italy in the year 79 CE. Hundreds of scrolls were covered under piles of ash. Although they survived intact, the documents are so fragile they can't be unrolled and read. Now a technique called computerized axial tomography might be able to scan the scrolls without damaging them. So the ghosts of buried Pompeii may finally have their say!

An ancient Persian ruler named Darius really used his head when he needed to send out a secret message. He shaved off a trusted messenger's hair and **tattooed a note** onto his scalp. Once the hair had grown back, Darius sent the messenger on his way. When he arrived at his destination, the messenger told the recipient: "Shave my head!" And the message was revealed!

MORE THAN MEETS THE EYE

Try this easy optical illusion for a real eye-popping showstopper!

MAGICAL MULTIPLYING MONEY

Some of us can make money disappear pretty quickly from our pockets. But you, the Magnificent Mintini, can make it multiply using nothing but a pencil!

YOU'LL NEED

Magician's Kit
(see page 7)

Trace the picture of the tuning fork shown here. Then copy it onto a piece of cardboard. Hold it up to your audience so your thumb covers the base of the prongs. Ask your audience to count the number of tines on this miraculous, self-altering fork. They should reply, "Three." Now hold your thumb over the tips of the tines. Now they see only two tines! A careful look at the illustration reveals that this fork shows two different perspectives at once. It's an optical illusion!

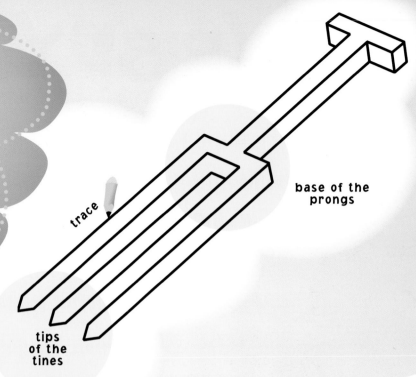

trace

base of the prongs

tips of the tines

I Tell your audience that you can make money appear out of thin air.

2 Choose a volunteer. Put two pennies on the tabletop about 5 cm (2 in.) apart.

3 Have the volunteer hold a pencil vertically halfway between the two coins, with the tip touching the table.

4 Tell your volunteer: "When I say the magic words, slowly move the pencil toward you. Keep looking at the pencil tip." Then say a spell: "Abracadabra. Penny times two. Make a new penny appear before you!"

5 As the volunteer moves the pencil, he or she will see a phantom penny appear between the real ones!

What's Going On?

At first, both eyes are clearly focused on three objects the same distance away. That's called the focal point. But as the volunteer moves the pencil closer, his or her eyes adjust to keep its tip in focus. The pennies slip out of focus. Each eye sees something slightly different, and images of the pennies overlap—creating the illusion of a third coin in between.

EYE SPY TRICKERY

This incredible illusion will leave your audience rubbing their eyes in disbelief.

THE GHOST IN THE BOTTLE

Conjure up a chattering ghost with an ordinary glass bottle.

BEFORE THE SHOW:

The day before your show, put the empty bottle in the freezer. It must be very cold for this trick to work.

1 Explain that you've caught a ghost. Ask your assistant to get the bottle from the freezer.

2 Turn the bottle upside down to prove it's empty. Explain that you will now coax the ghost to speak.

3 Dip your coin into the bowl of water. Explain that the ghost insists that the coin be clean.

4 Quickly place the wet coin over the bottle opening. The moisture will seal it in place.

5 Hold both hands firmly around the bottle. Say your spell: "Oh, great ghost, bring us your message from the other side!"

6 Keep speaking to the ghost. After about 20 seconds, the coin should begin bouncing and chattering!

YOU'LL NEED

Magician's Kit (see page 7)

~

empty glass bottle (without lid)

~

freezer

~

small bowl of water

~

friend to act as your assistant

What's Going On?

The heat of your hands warms up the "frozen" air inside the bottle. Hot air is lighter than cold air, so the warm air in the bottle starts to rise. Pressure from the rising air builds up under the coin until it pops! Then gravity pulls the coin back down with a clear "clink"!

PERFORMANCE TIP

Once the air temperature inside the bottle reaches room temperature, the trick will no longer work. So when the bottle is out of the freezer, work fast!

Mind-boggling Optical Illusions!

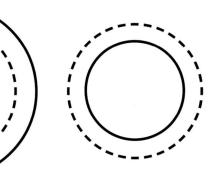

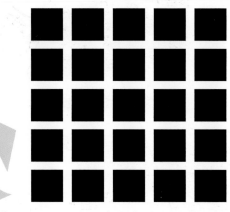

Do you see gray dots between these black boxes when you look at them? The dots aren't actually there. Your brain is confused by the black-and-white pattern, so it blends the colors together and you see gray spots.

Which dotted circle is bigger? Well, actually they're the same size. The difference in the size of the solid circles confuses your mind and makes it seem like the circle on the left is bigger. But grab a ruler and see for yourself!

Look at these two tables. Which one do you think is **wider**? That's a trick question because the tables are the same size and shape. Cover the legs and look at them again. This is an artistic illusion. It's just the angle of the tables that makes us think they're different.

THE MAGICIAN'S TOOLBOX

Magicians need to be experts in chemistry, physics, biology, and psychology to make their special effects work. Peek into their scientific toolbox to unveil some of their trickiest techniques.

I wonder where Harry is?

Hello, I'm right here.

Now You See It...

Magicians love to perform tricks that **fool your eyes**. For example, a magician will make a black object appear invisible by placing it in front of a black background. By using optical illusions, magicians seem to make the impossible possible!

It's All About Science

Talented magicians leave their audiences **baffled and bewildered**. That's because they focus on physics and use magnetism, air pressure, heat, and the effects of sound and light to impress.

Boggle That Brain

Magicians are masters at performing illusions that **fool your brain**. They know that there's always a slight delay between what your eyes see and when your brain knows about it. So they use this gap to make you think you see something that's no longer there or overlook something that is!

KA-BOOM!

You can be sure clever magicians know all about how to use chemical reactions to dazzle a crowd. For instance, mixing baking soda and vinegar is guaranteed to add a **dramatic effect** to a well-planned trick.

To: Brain

MENTAL MAGIC

Fake out your friends with this trick that makes you look like a mind reader!

I think some bunny's hungry.

BRING IT TO A BOIL

Use this magical truth-telling device to make water "boil"!

1. Tell your audience that you've turned an ordinary drinking glass into a lie detector. Fill the glass with water. Stop about 2.5 cm (1 in.) from the top.

Give It a Whirl!

Would you believe you can keep water in a container by swinging it around in a circle very quickly? To do this, you'll need a small pail with a handle and a spot outdoors where spills don't matter. Put some water in the pail and take it by the handle. Swing the pail around and around quickly, like a Ferris wheel. Funnily enough, the water won't come splashing out all over you. It'll be held against the inside of the bucket by a peculiar power called centrifugal force. You may have felt this same force working on you when riding certain amusement park rides.

2 Lay your handkerchief loosely over the glass, so the middle of the fabric dips into the water. Secure it with a rubber band.

3 Grasp the glass and handkerchief tightly. Quickly turn the glass upside down. Work over the bowl in case of any spills.

4 Now ask for a volunteer. Explain that if a liar touches the glass, the water will begin to boil.

5 Ask the volunteer his or her name. As the volunteer answers, have him or her touch the bottom of the glass. Nothing will happen.

6 Now ask the volunteer to answer the question with a fake name.

7 As he or she says the phony name, gently slide your fingers around the mouth of the glass. Pull the cloth tightly, making sure your audience doesn't see you do this. A bubbling brew will suddenly appear as the water "boils"!

What's Going On?

When you first turn the glass upside down, water molecules cohere, or stick together, to form a "skin" near the cloth. Air also pushes up under the cloth, holding it in place. But when you tighten the cloth, you increase the amount of space between the water and the cloth. This causes the air pressure inside the glass to decrease. The air outside the glass can now push up with a greater force. It pushes so hard that it briefly breaks the water's "skin." Air rushes into the glass before the skin can close up again. This air is seen as bubbles rising to the surface!

THE POWER OF PREDICTION

Leave members of your audience scratching their heads with a sneaky mind-reading trick.

Magician's Kit
(see page 7)

~

calculator
(optional)

764
−467
297

297!

I'VE GOT YOUR NUMBER

Who knew reading minds was as easy as 1...2...3?

1 Tell your audience that you can read minds. Choose a volunteer to help.

2 Give the volunteer paper and a pencil. Ask him or her to secretly write down any three-digit number, making sure all the numbers are different—467 is okay, but 221 is not.

3 Have the volunteer reverse the number (so 467 would become 764), then subtract the smaller number from the larger one.

4 Have your volunteer tell you only the last digit of the result. For example, since 764 - 467 = 297, the number would be 7. (They can use the calculator if necessary.)

5 Immediately announce the entire number to your stunned audience!

How Predictable

There have always been people who claim they can predict the future. One of the most famous was a French astrologer named Nostradamus who lived during the 16th century. He wrote a book of mysterious verses that many believe contains predictions about everything from events in history to the date when the world will end. Unfortunately for believers, Nostradamus' words aren't always very clear. And some say this means that they can be used to predict almost any occurrence.

What's Going On?

You can make your amazing prediction based on a number pattern. It just so happens that when you take a three-digit number, reverse it, and then subtract the smaller, the middle digit is always nine. (Try it!) Even more amazingly, the two outside digits always add up to nine. So when your volunteer tells you the last number in the answer, you automatically know the first digit—it's the difference between nine and that number (e.g., $9 - 7 = 2$). You also know the second digit will be a nine, and your volunteer just told you the third digit!

Famously Funny and Oh-So-Wrong Predictions

"This 'telephone' has too many shortcomings to be seriously considered as a means of communication."

From a memo written by the Western Union Company in 1876

"There is no reason anyone would want a computer in their home."

Ken Olson, founder of Digital Equipment Corporation, in 1977

"Everything that can be invented has been invented."

Charles H. Duell, Commissioner of the U.S. Office of Patents, in 1899

"Guitar music is on the way out."

Decca Recording Co., after refusing to offer a recording contract to The Beatles in 1962

"Heavier-than-air flying machines are impossible."

Physicist Lord Kelvin in 1895 – eight years before the Wright Brothers made the first manned airplane flight

MIND-READING MADNESS

You'll leave your friends speechless with these tricks that glimpse into their brains!

QUICK-CHANGE ARTIST

This mind-reading trick is priceless!

1 Give one dime and one nickel to a volunteer. Ask the volunteer to hold one coin in each hand. Turn your back so you can't peek.

2 Ask the volunteer to multiply the value of the coin in his or her right hand by 12. The volunteer should keep the answer a secret from you.

3 Now ask your volunteer to multiply the value of the coin in his or her left hand by 13. This answer should also remain a secret.

4 Finally, have the volunteer add the two figures together and subtract 7 from the total. Now tell the audience which hand holds which coin!

YOU'LL NEED

Magician's Kit
(see page 7)

Aw, he's twice the coin I am!

What's Going On?

Pay attention to how long it takes your volunteer to do the first two calculations. To multiply by ten—the value of a dime—you simply add a zero to the end of the number. But multiplying a number by five—the value of a nickel—takes longer. The quickest calculation is the hand with the dime. The rest of the calculations are just to distract the audience!

COIN CLAIRVOYANCE

You'll earn a big hand from your friends and family with this remarkable trick!

YOU'LL NEED

Magician's Kit
(see page 7)

1 Ask a volunteer to take a coin and hide it in one hand. Turn your back while this is being done.

2 Have the volunteer raise the hand with the coin above his or her head. Ask him or her to concentrate hard on the coin for about a minute.

3 Ask your volunteer to hold out both hands palm side up. Now quickly turn around. Tap on the fist that's holding the coin, and enjoy the applause when your volunteer reveals the coin inside!

What's Going On?

Blood is pumped through your body by your heart. It's harder for the heart to work against gravity. So when the hand with the coin is held above the head, it challenges the heart and less blood reaches the hand. After about thirty seconds, the coin hand appears lighter in color than the other.

NATURALLY MAGICAL

Magic doesn't just happen on center stage. Have a look at some of the magical mysteries you'll find in nature.

Going Up!

Tourists have been trying to defy gravity at **Magnetic Hill** in Moncton, New Brunswick, since the 1800s. At this magical mount, vehicles appear to roll up the hill on their own! But it's all an optical illusion. The land around the road appears to be an uphill slope, but it actually slopes downward. So while a car may look like it's going uphill, it's really rolling down!

Night Light

Have you ever witnessed the magic of the **northern lights**? This phenomenon, in which curtains of bright colors move across the night sky, is caused by the Earth's magnetic field. It pulls electrically charged particles into the Earth's atmosphere. These particles collide with gases, giving off bursts of energy that we see as waves of light. Enjoy the cosmic show!

The Nature of Magic

In ancient times, most people didn't have a clue as to what caused natural events such as the sun rising or rain falling. So to explain the unexplainable, they made up stories. For example, a bad storm was said to be the wrath of angry gods.

Spiritual leaders, called **shamans**, often claimed to have magical powers that they could use to please the gods and protect the tribe. To prove their supernatural abilities, shamans would perform amazing feats, like causing the sun to disappear during the day.

Shamans didn't really have magical powers—they just understood the workings of nature. Some knew that the planets and stars moved in predictable patterns, while others knew how certain chemicals interacted. By throwing in some theatrics like hypnotic drums and eerie lighting, shamans astonished their tribes. They were part magician, part scientist!

Welcome to the NORTH POLE

What a rebel.

The Real Sorcerer's Stone

Imagine a magical stone that, when spun, always comes to rest pointing in a north-south direction. Sorcerer's stones like these were discovered in China over 2,000 years ago. They're called **lodestones**, and they contain iron, a magnetic element. Since iron is attracted to the Earth's poles, a lodestone always points in a north-south direction.

GOING UP

You'll coax ice cubes to magically rise. And your audience will probably rise out of their seats, too!

THE LEVITATING ICE CUBE

Try this cool trick that's sure to lift your spirits!

YOU'LL NEED

ice cube

~

30 cm (12 in.) yarn or string

~

water

~

15 mL (1 tbsp.) salt

1 Put the ice cube on a clean, dry surface. Challenge your pals to pick it up using nothing but the string. If they give up, show 'em how it's done.

2 Wet the string with water. Lay it across the top of the ice cube. Sprinkle a tiny, quick shake of salt onto the cube and string. Wait about 10 seconds.

3 Grab both ends of the string and gently lift them up. Ta-da! The cube will stick to the string, allowing you to lift it without touching it!

Try This!

Adding sugar to water will also lower its freezing point. Repeat this trick using a spoonful of sugar for a really sweet effect.

What's Going On?

The secret is in the different melting points of fresh water and salt water. Fresh water, like a normal ice cube, freezes when the temperature drops below 0°C (32°F). But salt water won't freeze unless the water temperature is -2°C (-28°F). When you sprinkle the salt, it causes part of the cube to melt. The melted water runs across the cube, washing away some of the salt. Once the salt disappears, the water begins to freeze again—on and around the string. The string is then trapped in the ice and can be used to lift the cube into the air.

FUN FOR FRIENDS

Challenge your friends to perform this feat of magical prowess.
It may seem impossible, but it's not...for you!

SOUNDS LIKE MAGIC

The gasps from your audience will be just one of the sounds you'll hear in this trick.

YOU'LL NEED

Magician's Kit
(see page 7)

~

4 solid-colored plastic cups,
250 mL (8 oz.)

~

500 mL (16 oz.) water

~

small plastic toy that
will fit inside cup

1 Fill each cup with exactly 125 mL (4 oz.) of water. Make sure your friends agree that the cups are all exactly the same.

2 Blindfold one friend. Drop the toy into one of the cups. Challenge your volunteer to guess which of the four cups has the toy—without moving the cups or placing fingers in them.

3 Now it's your turn. While you are blindfolded, have your friend move the cups around.

4 Touch each cup in turn. Without being too obvious, tap each cup with your fingertip. Listen carefully. When tapped, the cup with the toy will sound different from the others.

5 Tell your friends which cup has the toy in it. Remove your blindfold to see their surprise!

TAP!

What's Going On?

Sounds are made when an object vibrates. How fast it vibrates determines its pitch— or how high or low it sounds. The faster the vibration, the higher the pitch. With the same amount of water, all four cups should each produce the same sound when tapped. The toy, however, raises the level of the water in the cup. That makes that cup vibrate more slowly when tapped, producing a deeper sound.

Try This!

By putting water in several cups at a variety of levels, you can produce all the sounds of a musical scale. Gather some cups and produce your own water harp!

29

FEELIN' THE PRESSURE

Who knew one balloon could cause such amazement!

THE VOODOO BALLOON

Stop the pop with your magical creation—the unpoppable balloon.
No matter how many pins you stick into it, the balloon will not break!
Warning: Check with an adult before using pins.

YOU'LL NEED
balloon
~
clear tape
~
pins

BEFORE THE SHOW:

Blow up your balloon until it's about two-thirds full. Tie it closed. Rip three or four small pieces of tape, about 2.5 cm (1 in.) long each. Stick each piece onto one side of the balloon. Make sure they're lying flat, so they're hard to see. If you want, reinforce each spot by using a second piece of tape to make a taped X.

1. Show your audience your magical balloon. Explain that no matter what, it will not pop.

2. To prove it, hold up a pin and show the audience. Stick the pin into the balloon through one of the pieces of tape. It doesn't pop!

3. Repeat with more pins, at the other places you have taped.

4. Then invite a member of the audience to test your balloon.

5. Without anyone noticing, turn the balloon so the side without tape is facing your volunteer. When he or she inserts the pin, the balloon pops!

6. Explain that perhaps it's not the balloon that's magic after all... just the magician!

Balloon Bits

Swiss balloon artist Ronald van den Berg fetched the world's speed record for making **balloon dogs**. This super speedster completed 100 pooches in 5 minutes and 46 seconds!

Gas station owner Kent Couch must have been having a slow day at the pumps. In the summer of 2007, he attached a **lawn chair** to 105 helium-filled balloons and flew it nearly 322 km (200 mi.) before landing in a farmer's field. His loony balloon journey lasted an incredible nine hours!

What a Memory!

Balloons are made up of a type of material called a polymer. Polymers contain molecules that are shaped like long chains. They intertwine like spaghetti on a plate.

This mixed-up mess makes polymers stretchy. So when you pull on a polymer, it expands. But when you let go, it snaps back to its original shape—like a balloon does when it deflates. This is called **shape memory**.

If a balloon is thick enough, shape memory may even cause its skin to seal up a tiny hole without the balloon breaking.

What's Going On?

The air inside a balloon is under more pressure than the air outside. Air under high pressure will move to areas of lower pressure if there is an opening—such as a pinhole. In a regular balloon, the air rushes toward the pinhole, forcing the balloon's rubber to tear. Pop! With your balloon, however, the tape stops a tear from forming—so no loud pop.

Try This!

Pierce the balloon down near the knot. With a little luck, it won't pop. Why? The balloon's skin is thicker near the knot since it is not stretched as much.

MAGICAL MOTION

Your audience will flip for these amazing card tricks.

Nooo! I'm not leaving!

PERFORMANCE TIP

It takes practice to perform this trick just right. Make sure your finger is perpendicular to the floor when it flicks the card.

THE STICKY COIN

Have you ever seen a trick where someone yanks a tablecloth off a table and all the dishes stay put? With a little bit of practice, you can do a version of this same trick.

YOU'LL NEED

Magician's Kit (see page 7)

1 Balance any playing card on the tip of your index finger. Then lay a penny on top, so it is resting exactly over top of your finger.

2 With the thumb and index finger of your other hand, sharply flick the edge of the card away from you. If you hit it just right, the card will shoot off your finger and the penny won't move a hair!

What's Going On?

When you flick the card, the energy from your finger is transferred to it. This makes it fly off your finger in a perfectly straight line. When done correctly, none of the energy will be transferred to the penny. So the penny will stay put!

FLIP IT!

Make a magic card turn upside down without touching it!

YOU'LL NEED

Magician's Kit
(see page 7)

1 Have a volunteer choose a card from your deck. Once your friend has memorized the card, have him or her place it on top of the deck.

2 Make sure your audience isn't sitting too close to your table. Explain that you are going to drop the entire deck and only the chosen card will magically land face up.

3 Straighten the deck of cards in your hands. While you are doing this, slide the top card over so about a third of it extends past the long edge of the deck. Keep your hand over the deck so the audience doesn't notice.

4 Hold the deck with your thumb on one side and your index finger on the other. Your grip should be very light.

5 Hold your arm outstretched about 50 cm (20 in.) above the tabletop.

6 Drop the deck. The secret card will land face up on the table!

What's Going On?

As the cards fall, a column of air rushes past them. It hits the secret card that's hanging over the deck. The air pushes up on this card, flipping it over before it lands on the table.

PERFORMANCE TIP

Practice this trick ahead of time to find the perfect height for dropping the cards. If you hold them too high or too low, your pal's card may not flip.

LET iT LEViTATE

Beat gravity in this suspenseful trick.

THE PHANTOM PAPER CLIP

Make an ordinary paper clip defy the laws of nature.

YOU'LL NEED

shoebox

~

strong magnet

~

construction paper

~

spool of thread

~

paper clip

~

clear tape

~

scissors

~

crayons, markers,
and paints

BEFORE THE SHOW:

Stand the box on its narrow end. Tape the magnet inside the box in the center of the top end. Tape construction paper over the magnet so it's hidden. Tie one end of the thread to the paper clip. Hold the paper clip near the magnet until you feel the attraction between the two. Move the paper clip down so it's as far as possible from the magnet, but is still attracted to it. Unwind the thread and tape it to the bottom of the box. Make sure the paper clip will "float" in the air. Decorate the box to make it look like a magical prop.

1 Show your audience the box, magnet side down. The paper clip will be swinging inside the box like a pendulum.

2 Explain that you have created a box that can defy gravity.

3 Wave your hands over the box and say your spell: "Abracadabra, abracadize. Make this paper clip rise, rise, rise!" With the back of the box to the audience, turn it over slowly until the paper clip is floating. Turn the box around and wow your audience!

What's Going On?

The magnetic force is strong enough to overcome the force of gravity. So the paper clip rises up, up, up!

magnet hidden under paper

paper clip

thread

tape

HERE WE GROW AGAIN

Convince your family and friends that you have
the wizardry to make flowers bloom.

FLOWER POWER

**Use your magic powers to make flowers
"grow" before an audience's eyes!**

BEFORE THE SHOW:

Make your flower.
• First, cut two flower shapes from a paper towel.
They should be slightly bigger than your palm. Poke a
hole in the center of each flower with your scissors.
• Lay one flower on top of the other.
• Roll another square of paper towel into a tight
cylinder. This will be the flower's stem.
• Stick one end of the stem through the hole
in each flower.
• Drip some red food coloring on the part of the
stem that is in the middle of the flower. Let dry.
• Cut the bottom of the flower stem so it is a little
taller than your glass. Squeeze your flower petals
together in your hand to make it look like the flower
has not bloomed yet.

YOU'LL NEED

2 paper towels

~

green and red
food coloring

~

scissors

~

drinking glass filled
with water

I Show your audience your white paper-
towel flower. Explain that you will make
this flower grow.

2 Put a few drops of green food coloring
into the water-filled glass.

3 Say a magic growing charm over the
flower: "Hocus-pocus, alakazow. Watch
this flower begin to grow." Then place
the flower in the glass. It will slowly start
to bloom and turn red! You may want to
perform another trick while you wait for
the flower to bloom completely.

Branch Out!

The largest known flower is a species of plant called *Rafflesia arnoldii*. It's found in the jungles of Indonesia, and its blooms can measure nearly 1 m (3 ft.) across and weigh in at up to 7 kg (15 lbs.)! But its **giant** size isn't the flower's only eye-opening feature. The speckled red blooms give off an **overpowering stench** that's said to smell like rotting flesh.

Bamboo **grows so quickly** that you can actually hear it getting taller! Certain species can grow as much as 121 cm (47.6 in.) in one day.

What's Going On?

You can thank something called capillary action for this trick. Water molecules are sticky. They cling to one another and to other surfaces. When the end of your stem touches the water, the green water molecules stick to it. They spread along the fibers of the paper, turning it green as they go. The uppermost water molecules pull on the molecules below them, dragging a watery chain behind them. When the water reaches the petals, it clings to the red food coloring. Soon, red water molecules spread along the petals, making your red flower bloom.

Wrap It Up!

Here's another trick that gets its magic from capillary action. You'll need a straw that comes in a paper wrapper. Rip off the end of the wrapper. Crumple the wrapper down around the straw tightly before pulling it off. Lay the crumpled wrapper on the table. Using the straw, place a drop of water onto one end of the paper. The wrapper will stretch out and grow, wiggling like a worm! Add more water to other parts of the wrapper to make it grow and wriggle even more.

MAGIC THROUGH THE YEARS

There's more to magic than meets the eye. Go back in time for a look at some magical history!

Goo.

It's in the Stars

The word "magic" comes from the Persian word *magus* (say: may-gus), meaning a follower of an ancient Persian religion. Some believed a magus had the ability to **change the future** based on what the stars said. Eventually, the term was used to refer to someone who was thought to be a sorcerer.

The Daily Star

Hoaxes and Hares

In 1726, a British woman named Mary Tofts tricked doctors into believing she'd given birth to rabbits! It was all a hoax, but Tofts's trick became well known. To take advantage of the publicity, a British magician came up with his own **rabbit trick**— pulling one from a hat. It's become one of the most famous magic tricks around.

Say the Magic Word

In ancient times, **abracadabra** was believed to be a magic word that protected magicians from disease. A magician often wore a pendant around his or her neck with the letters of the word arranged in a pyramid form. Starting at the top was the entire word. Then one letter was removed from each line. This was thought to be a way to drive out illness from the body.

Ahh...!

SKIN CREAM

BELLY CURE

FIRST-AID CREAM

MULTI-VITAMINS

TOOTH ACHE RELIEF

ABRACADABRA
ABRACADABR
ABRACADAB
ABRACADA
ABRACAD
ABRACA
ABRAC
ABRA
ABR
AB
A

winning lottery ticket

Long Live Magic

Prehistoric cave dwellers relied on sorcerers to ensure successful hunts. These **sorcerers** used illusions, such as making cave paintings appear to move, as part of their "magic show."

ODD ONE OUT

Everyone loves a good card trick, so give it your all with this one!

MYSTERY CARD HUNT

This odd trick will make even your most skeptical audience member believe in your magic powers!

YOU'LL NEED

Magician's Kit
(see page 7)

BEFORE THE SHOW:

Remove the face cards from your deck, and then split it into two piles—one with all the even-numbered cards and the other with just odd-numbered cards. Put the joker on top of one pile. Put the second pile on top of the joker. Place the deck of cards back in the box.

1 Show the cards to the audience, fanning them as you say: "I have here a regular deck of cards."

2 Divide the deck in half, using the joker as a marker.

3 Put the even cards face down in one pile, and the odd cards face down in a second pile.

4 Say to your volunteer: "When I turn my back, choose one card from either of the piles, memorize it, and put it anywhere in the other pile."

5 Give the volunteer time to choose, memorize, and replace the card in one of the piles.

6 Pick up the two piles and put them together. Fan the cards so you can see their faces but the audience can't. Pluck the secret card out of the deck and show it to your stunned audience.

Take a Turn!

Here's another trick that depends on odd and even numbers to work. Set three cups in a row. Place the two outer cups upside down and leave the middle cup upright. Then turn over the two cups on the left. Next, turn over the two outside cups. Finally, turn over the two cups on the left. All three cups will be upright. Challenge your friend to do the trick. But when you set up the cups, leave the two outer ones right side up and turn the middle one upside down. Your friend won't be able to match your magic skills!

What's Going On?

This trick relies on one of the simplest of number patterns—odd versus even numbers. When your volunteer takes the card from one pile and puts it in the other, he or she has unknowingly made sure that you'll be able to spot it in an instant. It will be either the only odd card in the even pile or the only even card in the odd pile!

CUT iT OUT!

Your audience will have to be especially sharp to figure out how you pull off this scissors trick.

GIVE YOURSELF A GOLD STAR

With one simple "snip," you'll be the star of the show!

YOU'LL NEED

gold-colored wrapping paper,
cut into a sheet measuring
22 cm x 28 cm
(8 1/2 in. x 11 in.)

~

scissors

1 Explain to your audience that you're going to give yourself a gold star for your performance so far.

2 Tell them: "I'll create a star in this piece of paper by cutting just one single, solitary line."

3 Fold the paper, as shown here.

4 Fold again, as shown.

5 Make two more folds.

6 Fold and unfold the paper on the dotted line.

7 Ask for a volunteer from the audience to help you.

8 Have your volunteer cut a single straight line along the fold you made in step 6. He or she will completely cut off the point of the folded paper.

9 Ask your volunteer to unfold the paper. It's a star—like you!

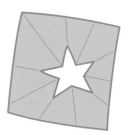

Starry Snippets

Polaris, sometimes called the **North Star**, is the only star that doesn't change its position in the sky with the seasons.

Shooting stars aren't really stars at all. These bright streaks of light across the sky are caused when small rocks called meteoroids crash into Earth's atmosphere. The collision creates so much heat that the rock burns up, leaving a sizzling trail in its wake.

What star can you often see in the **daytime**? The sun!

Why do **stars twinkle**? The particles in the Earth's atmosphere tend to bend light. The tiny back-and-forth movement of a star's light beams makes it seem as if the star itself is moving.

On a very dark night, you can sometimes see a white smear across the sky. That's part of the **Milky Way**, a star "neighborhood" that includes our own solar system. The Milky Way contains about one trillion stars!

The closest star to our solar system is called Proxima Centauri. This dim red star is over **four light years** away. That's over 40 million million kilometers (24 million million miles)!

What's Going On?

Geometry is your secret assistant in this trick. Each time you fold the paper, the layers circle around one point at the center of the page. The single cut ends up going through each of these five layers of paper, creating a symmetrical pattern—your five-pointed gold star!

Try This!

Experiment with different cuts to see what other shapes you can create. For example, if you fold your paper one more time, you can make a solid star inside a circle.

MAGICIANS OF THE PAST

Go behind the cape for a look at some of the most interesting magicians of all time!

I wish I could do that!

R.I.P

I'm Okay, Folks!

Benjamin Rucker performed in the early 1900s. His routine included being **buried alive**. Audiences would watch as he was buried inside a coffin. After several days, Rucker's assistants would dig him up and he'd step out, fit as a fiddle!

Micro-Magic

In 18th-century London, a well-known magician named Gustavus Katterfelto performed an eye-opening trick during his stage act. He'd make thousands of **tiny creatures** miraculously appear in a droplet of water. His magical prop? A microscope!

Ta-da!

There's No Locking Him Up

Magician and **escape artist** Harry Houdini could get out of all kinds of traps, including chains, ropes, and submerged boxes. How'd he do it? Houdini had great strength and flexibility. Plus, he was an expert at picking locks and always kept a tiny pick hidden from the audience.

Can I call you back? I'm a little tied up right now.

Got a Penny?

John Neville Maskelyne invented many popular tricks, including the **levitating woman**. But Maskelyne's talent for invention went beyond the stage. He also created the first pay toilet—a lock on the stall door was opened by inserting a penny.

NOW YOU SEE it, NOW YOU DON'T

Discover the secret of making objects appear and disappear in the blink of an eye.

THE DISAPPEARING PENNY

Make a coin vanish using nothing but water!

YOU'LL NEED

Magician's Kit
(see page 7)

~

pitcher of water

1 Tell your audience you have a bad habit of making money disappear before you can actually spend it.

2 Place a penny on the tabletop. Stand an empty glass on top of the penny.

3 Ask a volunteer if he or she can see the penny through the side of the cup. The answer should be yes. Make sure your volunteer is looking through the side of the glass, not down from the top.

4 Instruct your volunteer to keep his or her eyes fixed on the penny. As the volunteer stares at the coin, pour some water into the glass. The penny will jump and— poof!—disappear.

MISSING

Penny Spentwell
Disappeared
after magic show.
Last seen in piggy bank.

M
i
l
k

Fool Those Eyes!

Boo?

What's Going On?

Did you ever notice that when you put a straw into a glass of liquid, the straw seems to bend? That's because water bends light. This is called refraction. When your volunteer looks at the penny through the empty glass, he or she can see it plain as day. But when you pour in water, the light rays that are reflected off the coin are refracted away from your volunteer's eyes. So the coin seems to disappear!

A famous magic trick in the 1800s called **Pepper's Ghost** made ghosts appear on stage. To perform this trick, the magician angled a sheet of glass in front of the stage. An actor dressed as a ghost hid off stage, out of sight of the audience. When a light was shone on him, his reflection appeared in the glass, so the audience saw a flickering phantom frolicking on stage!

In 1983, magician David Copperfield made the **Statue of Liberty** disappear. The amazing trick was seen—or rather not seen—live on national television by millions of awestruck viewers.

In 1914, Harry Houdini made an elephant named Jennie disappear. Surprisingly, the trick, which was performed in New York City on one of the largest stages in the world, was **a flop**. It turns out the stage was too big and the elephant too far away from the audience. So instead of thinking Jennie had disappeared, many believed they just couldn't see her from where they were sitting.

MAGIC ON THE MOVE

Calling all wizards-in-training! Learn how to make objects move with these simple tricks that'll amaze your friends and family.

PEPPER BE GONE

Your magic skills can make pepper flee on your command!

BEFORE THE SHOW:

Dip one end of a skewer into liquid soap and let dry.

YOU'LL NEED

pitcher of water

~

pepper in a shaker

~

liquid soap

~

clear bowl

~

bamboo skewer, coffee stirrer, or other simple stick

1 Tell your audience that an evil wizard put a curse on you. The curse has made you repulsive. In fact, you can repel things with your touch!

2 Have your assistant fill the bowl with water. Ask him or her to shake pepper into the bowl until it covers the water's surface.

3 Ask the assistant to touch the tip of the skewer to the surface of the water. Make sure it's the soap-free tip. Nothing will happen.

4 Now take the skewer and touch it to the water, making sure you use the soapy end. Watch the pepper skitter away!

Run away! Run away!

What's Going On?

Water molecules cling together to form a skin on the water. Because pepper is light, it can sit on top of this skin. But the soap breaks the hold that the water molecules have on one another, so they pull apart. The pepper moves along with these molecules—away from the soap...and you!

SQUIGGLY WIGGLY WORMAGHETTI

Make your audience squirm as you turn skinny strands of spaghetti into wiggling, wriggling worms!

What's Going On?

When vinegar and baking soda are combined, they produce carbon dioxide gas—the same stuff that makes soda fizz. Gas bubbles stick to the spaghetti. And as the bubbles float to the surface, they bring the spaghetti along for the ride.

BEFORE THE SHOW:

Fill the bowl with water. Add the baking soda and stir until completely dissolved.

YOU'LL NEED

Magician's Kit (see page 7)

~

bowl of water

~

15 mL (1 tbsp.) baking soda

~

5 pieces uncooked thin pasta, like spaghetti

~

60–75 mL (4–5 tbsp.) vinegar

1 Explain to your audience that you're going to turn the spaghetti into worms. Have an audience member break the pasta into pieces that are 2.5 cm (1 in.) long.

2 Toss the pasta into the bowl of water and add your magic potion—a.k.a. the vinegar. As the water bubbles, say some magic words over the worms. Try "Presto wormo!"

3 Stir the worms with a spoon. Then cover the bowl with a handkerchief as you explain that it takes a few minutes for the worms to come to life.

4 Perform another trick. It will take 2 or 3 minutes for the spaghetti to start moving.

5 When the spaghetti begins to move, take away the handkerchief and let your audience behold the squirming spaghetti!

A REFRESHING SWITCH-A-ROO

Serve up a tasty surprise with this magical thirst-quencher.

PRESTO CHANGE-O

Prepare to baffle your friends with this trick that turns milk into water right before their eyes.

BEFORE THE SHOW:

Fill the plastic pitcher with the water until it's about two-thirds full. Put the plastic cup in the pitcher. Pour a little milk into it to help the cup float in an upright position.

YOU'LL NEED

Magician's Kit
(see page 7)

~

plastic pitcher
you can't see through

~

1–1.25 L (4–5 cups) of water

~

plastic cup or small bowl that
can fit inside the pitcher

~

another pitcher or jug, containing
about 250 mL (1 cup) of milk

1 Explain to your audience that you get thirsty during your magic show. Hold up the pitcher. Say that you like to drink milk during a show, but only once it's been poured from your special magical pitcher.

2 Carefully pour the milk into your prepared pitcher, making sure it goes into the plastic cup that's floating in the water.

3 Then lift the plastic pitcher and say a quick spell. Gently pour the "milk" into your drinking glass. Your audience will be amazed to see water instead!

PERFORMANCE TIP

Make sure the audience cannot see into your prepared pitcher when it's on your tabletop or when you are pouring from it.

Wet and Watery Facts!

An elephant can **smell water** that's several kilometers (miles) away!

Believe it or not, 97% of the **Earth's water** is in the oceans. Only 3% of this water can be used as drinking water. And 75% of the world's fresh water is frozen in the polar ice caps.

In a famous fable, a thirsty crow dropped stones into a pitcher of water to raise the level high enough so it could drink. Can crows perform this **mental magic** in real life? Of caw-se! Scientists at Cambridge University in England tested four crows by tempting them with a fake worm. The birds could see the worm at the bottom of a container of water but couldn't reach it. All four crows solved the problem by dropping stones into the container to raise the water level and bring the worm within reach.

About three-quarters of the **human brain** is made up of water.

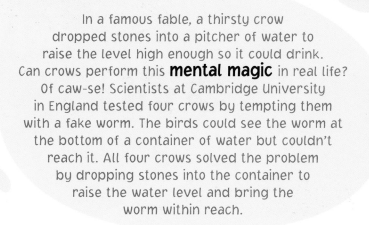

Cheers!

What's Going On?

This trick relies on a scientific principle called displacement. When you pour the milk into the small cup, it displaces, or pushes out of the way, the same amount of water. This causes the level of the water to rise in the pitcher. When you begin to pour, only water flows out of the spout. That's because the cup is lower than the spout, so milk doesn't escape!

GIVE IT UP FOR GRAVITY

You're really pulling out all the stops with this gravity-defying trick.

Flip Out!

Tell your friends that you can turn over a glass of water without spilling it. Fill the glass halfway with water. Completely cover the top of the glass with a playing card. Over a bucket—in case of a magic mishap!—quickly turn the glass over while holding the card in place. Now let go of the card. It will stay put and keep the water in the glass! This trick works because water molecules hold the card in place.

Look Up!

A man named Charles Blondin walked his way into history in 1859 by tiptoeing across the **raging torrents** of Niagara Falls on a tightrope! The rope was only 8.5 cm (3 in.) wide. Without a safety net to catch him, one misstep meant certain death. It took 20 minutes before Blondin reached the other side, but when he did, the crowd roared!

In May 2009, stuntman Steve Truglia **defied gravity** by driving upside down! He performed his topsy-turvy trick on the world's largest loop-the-loop track. With the help of an expert, Truglia worked out the exact speed needed to get his car all the way around the loop. And all his careful planning drove him right into the record books.

BALANCING ACT

Live on the edge! Astound your pals by balancing a drinking glass on the edge of a playing card.

YOU'LL NEED

Magician's Kit
(see page 7)

1 Tell your friends you can balance objects miraculously. Show them a playing card. Give them a plastic cup. Let them try to balance the cup on the edge of the card.

2 When your friends agree it can't be done, take the card in the hand you use for writing. Place your thumb on one vertical edge and your middle finger on the opposite side, so the card is facing the audience. The palm of your hand will be behind the card.

3 Raise your hand so the card is above the eye level of your audience.

4 With your other hand, lift the cup and set it on the card's edge.

5 Make a big show of it as you pretend to concentrate and try to balance the cup. Secretly slide your index finger up along the back of the card until the cup is resting on its tip. Let go of the cup. It's perfectly balanced!

Try This!

Consider adding a small amount of water to the glass to make the trick even more dramatic!

What's Going On?

This trick's secret has to do with the cup's center of gravity. That's an imaginary point around which an object's mass, or weight, is concentrated. Gravity works most strongly at this point; in other words, it pulls this spot down to the ground. Slightly tipping the cup, so it rests on your finger, shifts the center of gravity. It also allows the cup to be supported in two places.

WEIGHT FOR IT

These two tricks will leave your audience members scratching their heads in disbelief.

THE FORCE IS WITH YOU

Alchemists were magicians who claimed to turn lead into gold. But you, O Great Wizard, can turn yourself into lead!

YOU'LL NEED

a volunteer— the larger and stronger the better

1 Tell your audience that you have the amazing ability to make yourself as heavy as lead. So heavy, in fact, that no one will be able to pick you up!

2 Say a magic spell over yourself, such as "Weighty-shmeighty, kalamazoo! Make me strong and heavy, too."

3 Face your volunteer. Clasp your hands together close to your chest. It's important that you make sure your elbows jut out in front of you.

4 Ask your volunteer to lift you by the elbows. He or she won't be able to!

What's Going On?

Gravity keeps you glued to the ground. The way you hold your arms—with your hands up and elbows in front of you— shifts your center of gravity so that the force pulling down on you makes it almost impossible for most people to lift you up.

Try This!

Repeat this activity with a friend. But this time, keep your elbows right at your sides. Is it easier for your friend to lift you up now?

YOU "CAN" DO IT

Astound your audience by making one can of soda float, while an identical can sinks. It's absolutely uncanny how this trick works!

BEFORE THE SHOW:

Fill the bucket with cold water. Put the cans in the bucket.

YOU'LL NEED

bucket that's large enough to submerge a few cans of soda

cold water

large container

8 unopened cans of diet and regular soda

1 Explain to your audience that you have the ability to make items float or sink at will.

2 Remove a can of regular soda from the container. Show it to the audience, so they can see it's an ordinary, unopened can.

3 Drop the can into the bucket of water. It will sink.

4 Now grab a second can of soda from the container. Make sure the one you take is diet soda.

5 Say to your audience: "I'm going to make this soda can weightless." Wave your hand over the can and chant: "Presto change-o. Tip, tap, tight. Make this soda can extra light."

6 Then drop the can of diet soda into the bucket of water. It will float!

PERFORMANCE TIP

After finishing this trick, take away the water and cans quickly so no one has time to investigate.

What's Going On?

Regular soda contains sugar. Diet soda contains artificial sweetener. Sugar has a greater density, or is more compact, than sweetener. That means a can of regular soda is heavier than a can of diet soda. Plus, the density of the regular can is greater than that of water. So it sinks. Diet soda is less dense than water, so it floats!

MAGIC AT A GLANCE

There's no trickery here. Just more cool facts about the history of magic!

Pick a Card, Any Card

The first reports of **card tricks** date back to 14th-century Europe. They were performed by street artists who also specialized in activities such as juggling and sword swallowing.

Ring-a-Link

The Chinese Linking Rings, which is considered a classic illusion trick, was first performed in **China** around 2500 BCE. In this trick, magicians make it appear as if a series of solid metal rings link together or pass through each other. The number of rings used can vary from two to as many as ten.

JOKER

Tricked You!

The first written descriptions of magic come from ancient Egypt. Documents show that **Egyptian priests** performed magic tricks to convince people of their powers. For one trick, the sly priests used hidden mechanisms to make temple doors appear to open on command!

I knew that.

Really!
Do you mind?

One for the Books

During the Middle Ages, people believed that witches and their spells were real. But in 1584, a book was published proving that **witches' magic** was just an illusion. King James I of England had every copy of the book he could find burned in 1603!

CONJURING UP A SUCCESSFUL SHOW

Expert magicians don't leave any of their routine to chance. That means you'll need to put in plenty of prep time before you even get up on stage. Follow these simple guidelines to make sure your magic shows always bring down the house!

Before You Hit the Stage

★ Practice your tricks time and time again to be sure you can pull them off without a hitch.

★ Practice in front of a mirror. That way, you'll be able to see how your trick looks to your audience.

★ Ask a friend or family member to watch you do each trick and give you pointers on how to improve.

★ Don't rush your first performance. Hold off until you've perfected at least three or four tricks. A few amazing jaw-droppers make for a better show than a whole lot of sloppy tricks.

Tricks of the Trade

A great performance needs more than just nifty tricks. Keep these basic show-biz smarts in mind.

★ Keep your show short. Ten minutes is a good target for your first performance. Gradually increase your time on stage as your expertise grows.

★ Organize your tricks so that one seems to flow naturally into the next.

★ Save your most impressive tricks for the end of your act. There's a reason these are called showstoppers!

Dress for Success

Performers need to keep an audience's eyes on them. A colorful or unusual outfit is just the ticket to bring flair to your act. Consider these tried-and-true costume elements.

★ Make sure you're comfy. Your act will suffer if you're hot, itchy, or can't move freely. You need to focus on keeping an audience spellbound, not on your own discomfort.

★ You can't go wrong with the classic color combo of black and white. Choose a white shirt, black pants or a skirt, black shoes, and a black jacket. You can even throw on a snazzy bowtie, white gloves, and a homemade top hat to complete the look.

★ Consider including a scarf or handkerchief in your costume. It can be used in many tricks as well.

★ Get tricky with a secret pocket! Sew a hidden pocket in your shirt or jacket. It can be used to hide props.

It's Showtime!

★ Make eye contact with different members of your audience. This makes viewers more personally involved with your act, and they'll want you to succeed.

★ Slow it down. Most people speak too quickly when they first start performing. Make a conscious effort to speak more slowly, and don't forget to breathe!

★ Have fun! Audiences will sense your pleasure, and they'll naturally wind up sharing it.

THE SECRETS BEHIND THE SHOW

Want to make your show really stellar? Star magicians use these secret techniques to add extra sparkle to their acts. Follow their lead and your show will be a sure-fire hit!

It's Slightly Sneaky

Sleight of hand is a set of techniques that magicians use to quickly and skillfully execute a trick without an audience noticing. For instance, a magician may secretly get rid of a card right before an audience's eyes by moving his or her hands just so. Many consider this technique the most important skill for any successful magician.

You'll need to practice quite a bit to get the knack of fast fingers. That way, you'll be able to secretly discard a coin or switch a card's position from one hand to the other lickety-split. A great way to up your skill level is to try "piggybacking." That means you practice your sleight of hand while doing something else, like talking on the phone.

Try This!

The False Transfer may be one of the easiest sleight-of-hand techniques to master. Here's how to do it:

1 Hold a small ball with your right thumb and fingers.

2 Put the ball in your left palm.

3 Begin to close your left hand around the ball as you curl the fingers of your right hand around it.

4 Remove the ball from your left hand as it's closing. You'll have to act quickly so no one notices. It'll help if you distract your audience with a short joke or story.

5 The ball is now in your right hand. Open your left hand to show that it's empty. Then hide the ball with your right!

QUICK TIPS

Did you muff a trick? Laugh it off. Never let your audience see you sweat!

Resist the impulse to tell your audience what they are about to see. They'll be twice as astounded if they don't know what to expect.

Never do the same trick twice for the same audience...no matter how much they beg!

Perform every trick with energy and an air of excitement. Your audience will respond to your enthusiasm with excitement of their own.

Talk the Talk

Patter is an important part of every magic act. It's the words you say as you are doing your trick. This may include the story about how you learned the trick, where you found the materials, or how difficult it is.

Patter serves a few purposes. First of all, it entertains your audience. Second, patter can distract your audience from what you are doing. For instance, while you describe how you bartered for magic worms with an old warlock, your audience may not notice you slipping a coin into your pocket. Finally, patter fills in any gaps in your act—like while you're waiting for an effect to work.

For tip-top patter:

★ Practice your stories in advance so your words come easily and smoothly

★ Include short jokes—one-liners are best

★ Involve your audience by asking them questions

Shhhhhh...Don't Tell Anyone

Imagine you're on stage when suddenly an audience member stands up and says, "I know how you do that!" and then proceeds to reveal your technique. That sure would sink your act. Successful magicians, therefore, never reveal how they do their tricks. E-V-E-R.

This rule is so important that professional magicians even swear a special oath, promising to stay mum about their tricks.

Here's one version of the oath that you might want to take:

As a magician, I promise never to reveal the secret of any of my tricks to a non-magician, unless they also promise to uphold the Magician's Oath. I promise never to perform any trick without first practicing it until I can perform it well enough to maintain the illusion that I was using real magic.

SCIENCE CONCEPTS

You probably thought this book was just loads of fun. But, of course, it was loaded with lots of great science too. Here is a list of scientific topics covered in *Magic Up Your Sleeve*.

List of Magic Tricks

INDEX